Martin Luther King

by Sheila Rivera

Lerner Books • London • New York • Minneapolis

Photo Acknowledgements

The photographs in this book are reproduced with the courtesy of: © Carol Simowitz, p. 4; © Hulton-Deutsch Collection/CORBIS, p 6; © Bettmann/CORBIS, pp 7, 10, 14, 15, 19, 20, 22; Archives Collection, Birmingham Public Library, Birmingham, AL, p 8; Library of Congress, p 11; © The Illustrated London News, p 12; © Washington Post; reprinted by permission of the DC Public Library, p 16; © Flip Schulke/CORBIS, p 17; National Archives, pp 18, 24; © Ted Spiegel/CORBIS, p 25; EyeWire by Getty Images, p 26.

Front Cover: © Bettmann/CORBIS.

First published in the United Kingdom in 2009 by
Lerner Books,
Dalton House,
60 Windsor Avenue,
London SW19 2RR

Website address: www.lernerbooks.co.uk

This edition was updated and edited for UK publication by Discovery Books Ltd., First Floor, 2 College Street, Ludlow, Shropshire SY8 1AN

Words in **bold type** are explained in a glossary on page 31.

British Library Cataloguing in Publication Data

Rivera, Sheila, 1970-
  Martin Luther King - 2nd ed. - (Pull ahead books.
  Biographies)
    1. King, Martin Luther, Jr., 1929-1968 - Juvenile
  literature 2. African Americans - Biography - Juvenile
  literature 3. Civil rights workers - United States -
  Biography - Juvenile literature 4. African American civil
  rights workers - Biography - Juvenile literature
  5. Baptists - United States - Clergy - Biography - Juvenile
  literature 6. African Americans - Civil rights - History -
  20th century - Juvenile literature
  I. Title
  323.1'196'073'092

ISBN-13: 978 0 7613 4373 8

Printed in Singapore

Table of Contents

People celebrate Martin Luther King Day.

Martin Luther King Day

In January, Americans **celebrate** a holiday called Martin Luther King Day. This holiday was named after a special American. Do you know why they celebrate this day in his honour?

Martin Luther King had big dreams for the people of the United States.

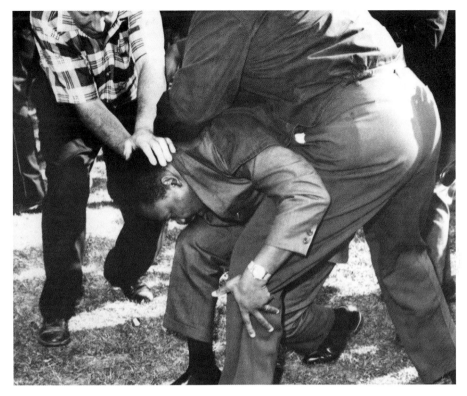

These men tried to stop Martin from speaking.

Some people tried to stop Martin from making his dreams come true. They did not agree with his ideas. But Martin never gave up. He was **determined.**

Only white people could sit in the front of the bus.

Unfair Treatment

When Martin was growing up, black people did not have the same rights that white people had. Laws said that black people could not sit with white people in restaurants or on buses.

Only black students went to this school.

Black children and white children could not go to the same schools.

Martin saw that African Americans were treated unfairly.

Blacks had to use doors marked 'colored'.

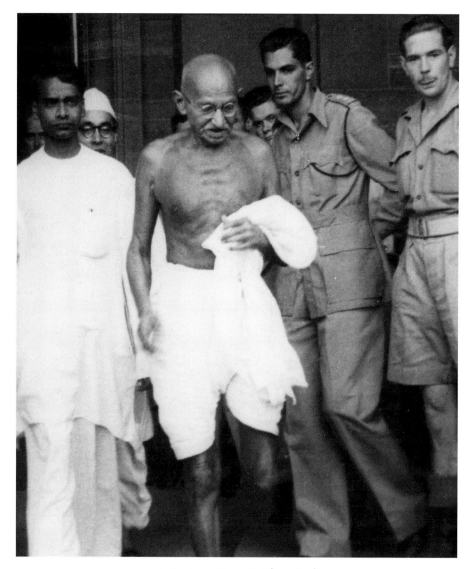

Mahatma Gandhi (centre)

Peaceful Ways

When Martin grew up, he read about a man named Mahatma Gandhi. Gandhi lived in India. He did not believe in fighting. He taught people how to **protest** against unfair treatment in peaceful ways.

Martin wanted to help black people.

Martin liked Gandhi's ideas. Martin
was determined to help black people in
the United States.

14

He showed people how they could work to get fair treatment without fighting.

These people wanted schools to let in both blacks and whites.

Martin gave speeches about the unfair way that blacks were treated. He talked about peace.

He said that everyone should be
treated the same. A person's **race**
or skin colour should not matter.

People marched for equal rights.

Martin led people on peaceful **marches.** They demanded fair treatment for everyone.

Some white people did not want blacks to have the same rights as whites. They attacked the marchers.

Some white people shouted at the marchers.

Police officers take Martin to jail.

Determined to Help

Some people were angry at Martin. The police **arrested** him many times. But they didn't stop him. Martin was determined to make change peacefully.

Martin gives his 'I have a dream' speech.

Martin's Dream

Martin gave a famous speech in Washington, DC, on 28 August 1963. He said, 'I have a dream that one day little black boys and black girls will be able to join hands with little white boys and white girls as sisters and brothers'.

Martin won the **Nobel Peace Prize.**

The prize is a great honour. It is given to someone who works for peace.

Martin received a Nobel Prize Medal like this one.

Now all people can work and play together.

Changing the World

Martin's determination helped change unfair laws. He taught people that they could change the world in peaceful ways. That is why Americans celebrate Martin Luther King Day.

Martin Luther King Timeline

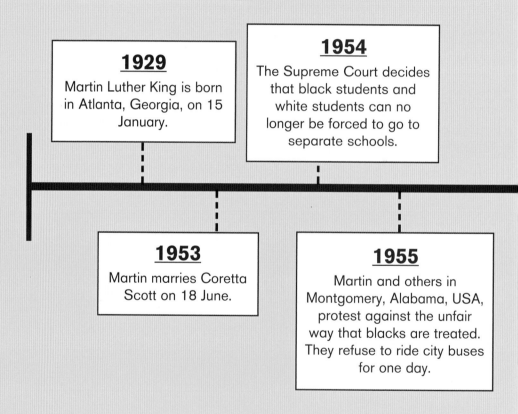

1929

Martin Luther King is born in Atlanta, Georgia, on 15 January.

1954

The Supreme Court decides that black students and white students can no longer be forced to go to separate schools.

1953

Martin marries Coretta Scott on 18 June.

1955

Martin and others in Montgomery, Alabama, USA, protest against the unfair way that blacks are treated. They refuse to ride city buses for one day.

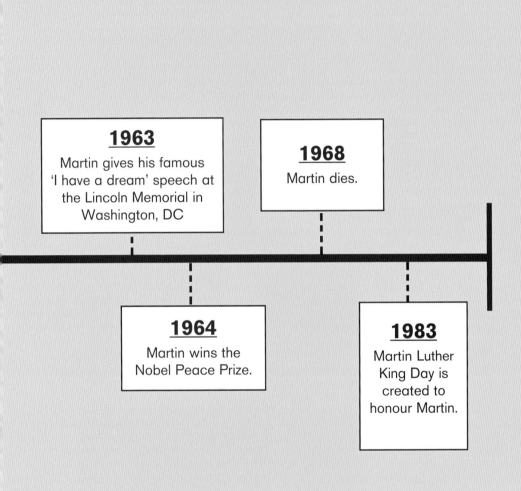

1963
Martin gives his famous 'I have a dream' speech at the Lincoln Memorial in Washington, DC

1968
Martin dies.

1964
Martin wins the Nobel Peace Prize.

1983
Martin Luther King Day is created to honour Martin.

More about
Martin Luther King

● Martin studied hard and began college when he was only fifteen years old.

● When Martin won the Nobel Peace Prize, he received $54,000. He gave some of the money to groups who supported equal rights.

● Martin Luther King Day is celebrated on the third Monday of January every year. This day was chosen because it is close to Martin's birthday.

Glossary

arrested: taken to jail by the police

celebrate: to have a party or do another activity to honour a special occasion

determined: to be firm in sticking to a purpose

marches: groups of people walking together for a purpose

Nobel Peace Prize: an honour given for a person's work for peace

protest: to express strong disagreement

race: physical traits shared by a group of people that are passed on from one generation to the next

Index

First published in the United States of America in 2006
Text copyright © 2006 by Lerner Publishing Group, Inc.